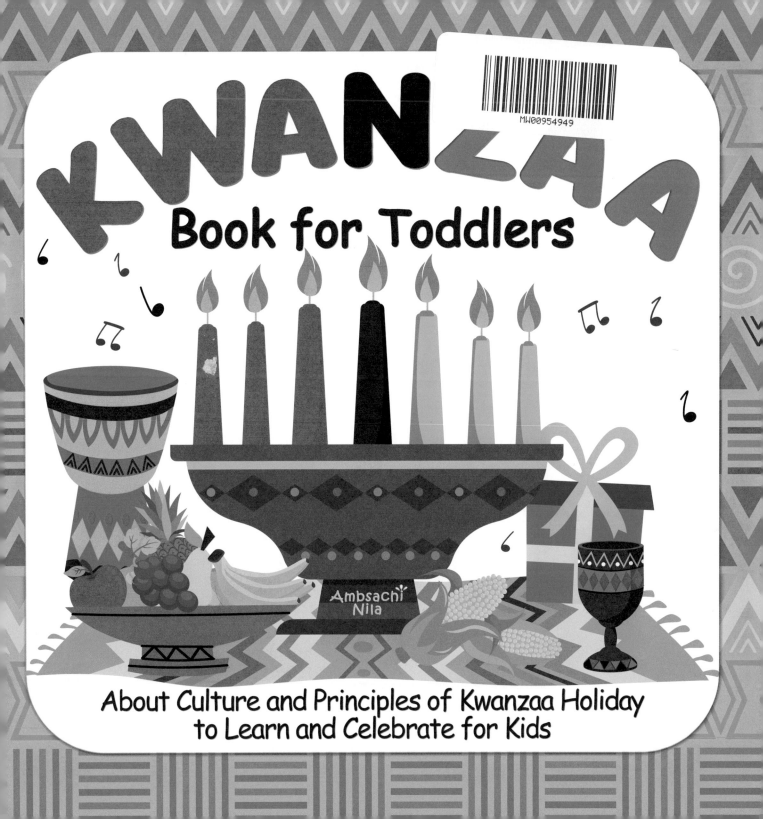

KWANZAA
Book for Toddlers

Ambsachi Nila

About Culture and Principles of Kwanzaa Holiday
to Learn and Celebrate for Kids

PUBLISHED IN 2024 by Ambsachi Nila

Copyright by Ambsachi Nila.

KWANZAA

is a holiday for all Africans and African-Americans.
We celebrate our history, culture and unity.
No matter what faith,
all Africans can celebrate Kwanzaa. And they do!

The word Kwanzaa comes from the East African Swahili language.

KWANZAA

really means:

First Fruits
HARVEST TIME

In Africa and many other places, people celebrate the harvest and give thanks for it.

Kwanzaa holiday was established in 1966 by Professor Maulana Karenga.

It lasts
7 days

Kwanzaa is a week-long holiday celebrated every year from December 26th to January 1st.

Kwanzaa Holiday honors our family, community, values, culture and history!

Habari gani?
(hah-BAR-ee GAH-nee)

This is a **Swahili** greeting and it means: What's new?

Kwanzaa is a very joyous holiday! Each day of the holiday we celebrate one of **The Seven Principles** of Kwanzaa that are called: **Nguzo Saba**

Celebrating Kwanzaa is special
that's why we have some UNIQUE symbols
with important meaning for this holiday.
Let's get to know them!

Kinara is a **candle holder** made of wood.
The Kinara holds seven candles
- three red, one black and three green.

Mishumaa Saba
(mee-shoo-MAH-ah SAH-bah)

is seven candles. Each candle symbolizes one of the seven principles of Kwanzaa. We light one candle each day.

Kinara
(kee-NAH-rah)

Mkeka is the Kwanzaa mat placed on the table.
Then we place the other important items on it
while celebrating Kwanzaa.
It is a foundation of our tradition and history.

MKEKA
(m-kay-kah)

Kikombe Cha Umoja

(kee-KOM-bay chah oo-mo-jah)

The Kwanzaa Unity Cup

The Unity Cup symbolizes
honoring and thanking our African ancestors.

Mazao The crops (Mah-ZAH-oh) are fruits and vegetables symbolizing the end of the harvest. Try to name them all!

Mazao are the basis of Kwanzaa,
symbolizing the African harvest festival,
which is the result of the collective, productive work
of the entire community.

Muhindi
(moo-HEEN-dee)

are ears of corn that are intended
for each child in the family.
They are placed on Mkeka.

The gifts we give each other during Kwanzaa symbolize promises made and kept.
We call them:

ZAWADI
(zah-WAH-dee)

Nguzo Saba

(n-GU-zo SAH-bah)

is a supplemental symbol.

These are seven principles written in **Swahili** language.

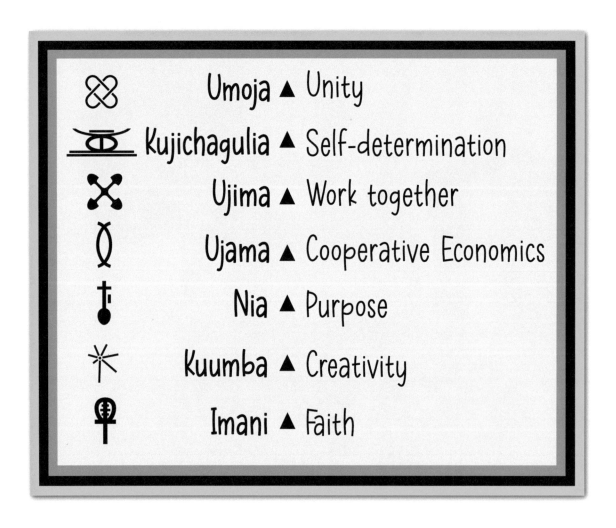

Umoja ▲ Unity

Kujichagulia ▲ Self-determination

Ujima ▲ Work together

Ujama ▲ Cooperative Economics

Nia ▲ Purpose

Kuumba ▲ Creativity

Imani ▲ Faith

BENDERA

(bayn-day-rah)

is the Flag, which is also the supplemental symbol
on with each color representing something different:

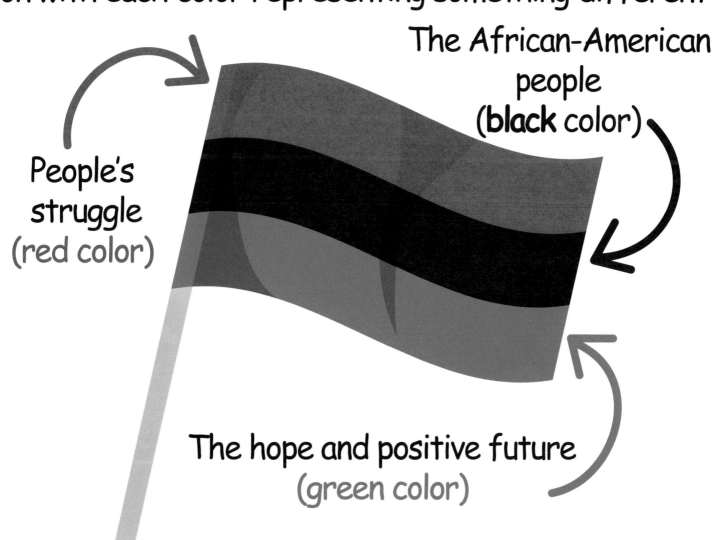

The African-American
people
(**black** color)

People's
struggle
(red color)

The hope and positive future
(green color)

1 DAY

UMOJA
(oo-MOH-ja)

Unity

It is the first principle we celebrate on the first day of Kwanzaa.

On this day we light the first candle on the kinara. It is a day of unity of the family, community and nation. We often visit each other and help others if they need it. This is a way to show our unity.

KUJICHAGULIA
(koo-jee-CHA-goo-lee-ah)

Self-determination

On the second day of Kwanzaa we light a red candle.
This principle means deciding who you want to be,
what you want to do in order to define
and name ourselves, to create for ourselves.

KWANZAA

3 DAY

UJIMA
(oo-JEE-mah)

Working Togheter and Responsibilty

On the third day of Kwanzaa we light a green candle. It's a principle that calls for building together and reminds us that everyone is responsible for our community.

UJAMAA
(oo-jah-MAH)
Cooperative Economics

This principle means supporting African-American businesses. We want our own stores and businesses to grow so we use their services and shop at them. On the fourth day we light another red candle.

5 DAY

NIA
(NEE-ah)
Purpose

On the fifth day of Kwanzaa,
we celebrate the common concern
of building and developing our community.
We read books about our heroes.
Maybe one day you will achieve something great
and become a hero for your community.

On this day we light
another green candle.

6 DAY

KUUMBA
(koo-OOM-bah)
Creativity

This is the day we decorate our homes for Karamu. We try to do our best to make our community more beautiful and beneficial than we found it.

KWANZAA

On this day we light the last red candle.

KARAMU
(kah-RAH-moo)

Karamu is a feast where families celebrate
with friends and relatives.
After dinner we sing, tell stories,
dance and play African drums!

There is plenty of delicious African food on our table!
We eat gumbo, smothered ribs and okra stew,
collard greens, jerk chicken, jollof rice,
sweet yams and more!

There are also desserts such as coconut cake
or cornbread. Everyone takes a sip from the unity cup!

IMANI
(ee-MAH-nee)
Faith

It's the last day of Kwanzaa!
Imani means believing with all our heart in ourselves
and others, in our family, the future and the past.
On this day we talk about being joyful
and being our greatest believers all year long!

On the seventh day,
we light the last candle on the Kinara.

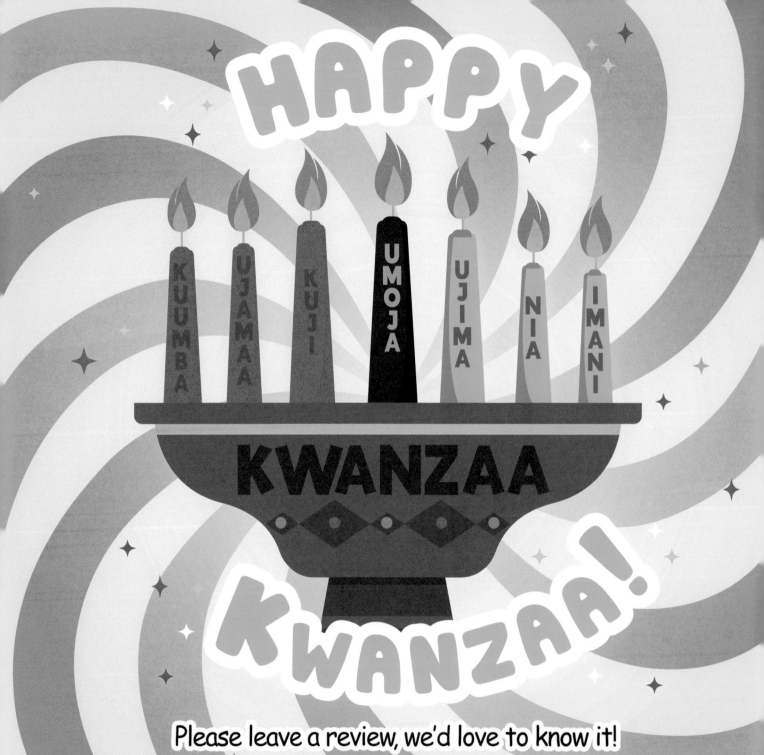

Please leave a review, we'd love to know it!

25992816R00021